THE RENUNCIATIONS

Also by Donika Kelly

Bestiary

THE
RENUNCIATIONS

Poems

DONIKA KELLY

Graywolf Press

This publication is made possible, in part, by the voters of Minnesota through a Minnesota State Arts Board Operating Support grant, thanks to a legislative appropriation from the arts and cultural heritage fund. Significant support has also been provided by Target Foundation, the McKnight Foundation, the Lannan Foundation, the Amazon Literary Partnership, and other generous contributions from foundations, corporations, and individuals. To these organizations and individuals we offer our heartfelt thanks.

Published by Graywolf Press
212 Third Avenue North, Suite 485
Minneapolis, Minnesota 55401

www.graywolfpress.org

Published in the United States of America

ISBN 978-1-64445-053-6

2 4 6 8 10 9 7 5 3

Library of Congress Control Number: 2020944389

Cover art: Lorna Simpson. *Blue Dark*, 2018. Ink and screenprint on gessoed fiberglass. 102 x 144 x 1⅜ in (259 x 365.8 x 3.5 cm). © Lorna Simpson. Courtesy of the artist and Hauser & Wirth. Photo credit: James Wang. Cover design: Jeenee Lee Design

With gratitude for Elizabeth, Carlisha, Ama, and Heather

Contents

THE RENUNCIATIONS

To live past the end of your myth is a perilous thing.

Anne Carson

House of Air, Hours of Fire

I was born into a house of air,
my dad born to bear, to share, his burden.
I was his dominion, a bit of land
turned to use. Where he plowed, I was worn,

and where worn, I strained. I knew little
of the life behind the hand that sounded me,
that turned the field, that planted the maze,
yet I answered to his name as if it were my own.

Then came the fallow, when I came into my body
as a horse, as a bird, as a beetle scurrying
in the brush. For many seasons, I was known by his
name but rarely worked by his hand. The field receded,

overgrown. Then came the hours of fire, her joy
at my taking her name—one given to her mother
and taken by her—the undergrowth charred to ash.
In the distance, a house, neither mine nor his.

Was I happy? Happier, yes, to have some sky,
to see the horizon, to want to know my body
unworked. I lived in the flame, practiced being
incomplete, a progression, an action without place.

I once thought it a carapace I shed,
that house, that name, my time as a field,
but I think of the fire, the brief time
I will have held her name, this one shell taken

for another, and I know I am palimpsest.
I house the air, the earth, and flame—though nearly anything
can be overwritten, and what can be left behind
is no more or no less a matter of will.

Now

Dear—

The　grown woman

remembers

when she breaks

a woman　to

save herself.

9

Dear—

We come from abundance, each season
bowed with rain. But here is the earth,
eager to flame, the air like salt, thirsty
even for the water we carry
in our skin. New wanderers in this land,
we do not know how to wait for water,
have never waited so long for rain
that every tree died, left to stand tinder.

For now, I watch the shoulder burn,
drive through the smoke that blots the mountains,
and holds the old yolk of sun. I know nothing
of fire, its reach, its spread, know only
that every body makes its own ash,
manages its own diminishing.

Bedtime Story for the Bruised-Hearted

The trees were all women once,
fleeing a god whetted with lust

until their fathers changed them, bound
their bodies in bark, and still the god took:

a branch to crown his own head,
the reeds to hold his breath.

How like them, our fathers,
those small gods who unearthed

their children with rage,
who scored the bark

and bent the branch
to bind their bodies with our own.

Tonight, my love, we are free
of men, of gods, and I am a river

against you, drawn to current and eddy,
ready to make, to be unmade.

Ars Empathica

Muir Woods National Monument

We lived in the imperative:

Walk through the tree.
Spin in the light.

Take dominion
over one another.

But about the tree—
no euphemism there:

A tree fell.
A man with metal teeth

ate the bark,
                    the heartwood,
the bark.

We were like that then,
eaten and eating,

sawing and sawn.
I mean, of course, our bodies,

but also how we mounted,
together, the hill:

Be dizzy, said the sun.
Be dizzy, said the blood.

Be dizzy, said the heart and lungs and vessels between.

How I cried at the summit.
You blocked the sun

and, somewhere, the ocean.
What sweet anchor your eyes made.

The Last Time

I hardly remember the last time
we touched each other with tenderness:

the evening's fall, the light dim, the rug new,
our life rambling ahead of us as the valley runs

to the foothills. Surely I called your name,
pulled you close; surely you trembled, our bodies

tangled and damp; yet what lingers in my mind,
what rings so clear is the hot mouth of shame opening

in my gut, awakened by the more I'd wanted: to taste
and at the same time be tasted, to be ridden, to take

inside me whatever you would give. Shame,
in both the wanting and the wanting's return,

swallowing whatever longing I wanted to voice.
I could hardly know that mouth's alarm,

gilding the night, was a warning—had assumed
the maze farther south, its center quiet.

Love Poem

Let us be ocean and coast, a taking
into and over one another:
shifting sediment, a breaking down

of rock: dredge and deposit. A series
of prepositions meaning proximity,
although the most of us extends away

from one another. Once, in winter,
I ventured far inland, forgot the crash
of gravity pulling you over me

and away—forgot there is a place
where we meet and retreat but never let go.
Let this be a moment of remembering,

my love, as I stand at the edge of myself,
cliff and sea grass and the screaming gull above,
sighting your breadth to the horizon.

Continental Drift Theory

For two nights we slept
as two people who were once
in love: our bodies

settled into one another,
our skin quiet. No quickening,
only habit, and sleep hard come.

Our first farewell, said
without knowing, drowned
by our delight, shared and singular,

in what surrounded us:
the otter smashing some meal
against the pilings;

the little red crabs
sweeping backward
under the boardwalk;

the line of pelicans
cutting low above the harbor.
That April afternoon,

the light bending long
across the water, did I not think,
my love, there at the moment

the ending began like a rock
slipped into the bay?
I'd wanted to fix in my mind

your face, wanted to fix,
at the coast, the slow drift
that separated us.

Difficult now to imagine—
the gesture weak,
the occasion quite late.

Cartography as an act of remembering

My hand scales each elevation, every
depression, sounds each body of water,
however small, and folds into the river
that runs my palm the smell of your neck,
the animal nuzzle of cheek to cheek,
to keep with me when you are away.

You are away. I hunt your scent, your skin,
practice resurrection in the palm of my hand,
unfold you over the uneven terrain
of my own body in the dark. Where cosmos,
where starless sky, where wind and summer night,
I bend into the arc of you, which is me
trying to remember your mouth on mine,
your breath in my ear, my name blowing past.

In the Chapel of St. Mary's

I can't tell you what happened
there, why I entered the sanctuary,

a nonbeliever. Only that I
have been thinking about worship,

the altar of the body and supplication,
for some time. My thoughts turn,

as they often do in this season of absence,
to my wife, and how tired a god can get

when called, and too often, for little reason
but loneliness. Of course, I don't mean *god* here,

but rather the woman I love, who alters
the orbit of my life, pulls me with the density

of light toward her, the draw thinner
when she is farther away, as she is now.

I try to find comfort in the inevitability
of science, when what I lack is faith.

The sanctuary—the stained glass,
four girls saturating it with soft chatter,

small pots of stargazer lilies, a lace ribbon
for each pew—this place is full of faith

in the unknown, and I don't know
how to believe in what I cannot see.

Tonight, I will drive through the foothills
and into the valley. I will try to make

a little practice, to trust you are with me,
even though you are somewhere else.

Then

Dear—

I wonder what kind of ▮ animal

swells and breaks

23

Oracle

The god in my brain
is no god, only a homunculus
I recognize as myself.

The god in my heart,
the same. The god of my liver,
the same. The god

of my guts and thin skin:
me. The homunculus
guiding my father

bears his mustache
and heavy-lidded eyes.
Was it he who placed

the god in me that is me?
And what do I mean
by *god*, I wonder.

I take my questions
to the oracle,
say either:

Who placed the god in me?
or
What do I mean when I say god?

The reply to both
being, *Your father.*
Stupid oracle, I think.

Fathers are for children,
and I was never a child,
only a smaller image of myself.

Donika Questions the Oracle

Who hid my dad in the mountain,
impoverished, where he would remain,
invisible and rationed, not on milk and honey,
but on bologna and saltines, until he grew
strong enough to kill the father?

Which father?

Do I mean his daddy, exiled for the rest
of his diabetic days to a closet
in a house with no power, no water,
where my dad—his sisters and his brothers
caught for a time by the crack rock and the pipe,
lighting up in the dark—lived?

Surely not his daddy, oracle, surely not.

How long was he the youngest? How long
was he a child? What god swallowed him
whole? The god, perhaps, who split
his mother in two? Or took his brother
with a bullet from another father's gun
in the sunlight in the afternoon?

Did he really hold his dying brother's hand,
oracle, the brother who wanted
only an apology on my dad's behalf?

Who held him when his mother died?
Who told him of a heaven where dead
mothers and brothers go?

O, the pigeons!

What of the pigeons, oracle? Did he tend them,
watch them rise from the roof of the house
with no power or water, but a daddy in a closet,
his sisters and brothers flaring in the rock light?

Did he delight in their return? The pigeons,
I mean? Did he ever delight, oracle, in anything
a child might? Did he look for his name in the sky?
Did he ride a bike, made from junk parts,
in the South Central LA sun as fast a boy might?

Surely he did that, oracle, surely that.

And when he rose like an improbable stone
from the father's gut—whichever father
I mean here, whichever father makes sense—
the siblings, the pigeons, his daddy in exile,
his name in the sky—when he rose, with the stone
of himself in his hand, covered in bile and mucus,
free now of someone more powerful
than the child he surely once was,
did he know the terrible thing he would become?

The Oracle Remembers the Future Cannot Be Avoided

Los Angeles, California, 1970s

The oracle remembers
the cloudless quality of the day.

Remembers the boy, his hand
lost in his brother's hand.

The brother, the oracle remembers,
is tall and soft-haired.

He and the boy share this softness.
The boy hurts: another boy

has seen everything he can't control
and called out to the yard—

[   ]!

His brother, the oracle knows,
wants only to make right the seeing.

The oracle watches them walk,
can bear this part of remembering,

the walking across an alley
bordered with empties—

forty-ounce Olde English, Colt 45,
cans of Cactus Cooler, candy wrappers—

to the apartment complex,
the moment nearly upon us.

Is there a breeze?
Does a cloud appear?

The oracle turns from the knock.
The opening door—

A father with a gun in his belt.
The gun in his hand.

      The trigger pulled.

The boy holds his brother's hand.
The boy cries.

And as the oracle turns, still, away,
the brother bleeds out, lets the boy go.

My Father Visits the Oracle Before I Am Born

He expects a vision
of his own death. Body opened,

as his mother's:
abrupt and with mercy.

He expects the barrel of the gun.
He expects exile in a closet.

He expects, in short,
a truncated life.

By now he knows intervention
is only postponement.

He asks,
[   ]?

And the oracle answers:
[   ].

Afterward and forever,
he disavows his body
as something he can control.

Portrait of My Father as a Winged Boar

When his mother dies—by metal
turned slicing blade—from her
blood springs my father,

whose name I refuse
to say as he refuses
his father, the half-known man

who sired him. In the dry LA light,
the boy, my father, turns
so that he is caught—

one way: a winged boar—
another: a giant,
a gold blade of a man—

both high-skulled, thick-maned:
a juvenile without a sounder,
a boy without a mother.

He recognizes himself
only in the man, carves
himself into golden armor,

but the rutting
fact of him—the curved
tooth, the thick neck

and beating wings—trembles
beneath his skin. Whatever sheen
the California sun

burnishes out of his body,
whatever good work
his thickening hand

compels, whatever woman
he touches in the afternoon,
on the roof, he cannot deny

his firstborn, his red fledgling,
her many heads and hands.
What he makes for her:

a junk bike she loves   cattle   red

        in the field   a mirror

a red wreckage of her body.

Sanctuary

The tide pool crumples like a woman
into the smallest version of herself,
bleeding onto whatever touches her.

The ocean, I mean, not a woman, filled
with plastic lace, and, closer to the vanishing point,
something brown breaks the surface—human,

maybe, a hand or foot or an island
of trash—but no, it's just a garden of kelp.
A wild life.

This is a prayer like the sea
urchin is a prayer, like the sea
star is a prayer, like the otter and cucumber—

as if I know what prayer means.

I call this the difficulty of the nonbeliever,
of waking, every morning, without a god.

How to understand, then, what deserves rescue
and what deserves to suffer.

Who.

Or should I say, what must
be sheltered and what abandoned.

Who.

I might ask you to imagine a young girl,
no older than ten but also no younger,
on a field trip to a rescue.

She is led to the gates that separate
the wounded sea lions from their home and the class.
How the girl wishes this measure of salvation for herself:

to claim her own barking voice, to revel
in her own scent and sleek brown body, her fingers
woven into the cyclone fence.

From *The Catalogue of Cruelty*

Once, I slapped my sister with the back of my hand.
We were so small, but I wanted to know

how it felt: my hand raised high across
the opposite shoulder, slicing down like a trapeze.

Her face caught my hand. I'd slapped her in our
yellow room with circus animals

on the curtains. I don't remember
how it felt. I was a rough child.

I said *No.* I said *These are my things.*
I was speaking, usually, of my socks:

white, athletic, thin and already gray
on the bottom, never where I left them.

I was speaking of my fists raining down
on my brother's back. My sister's. Socks.

In the fourth grade, in California,
I kicked Charles in the testicles. At that school,

we played sock ball: hit the red playground ball
with the sides of our hands and ran the bases.

I kicked Charles with the top of my foot, caught him
in the hinge of ankle. I wanted to see

what would happen. I didn't believe
anything could hurt like it did on TV.

Charles folded in half at the crease of his waist.
My god, I was a rough child, but I believed

Charles, that my foot turned him to paper.
Later, I kicked my dad the same way,

but he did not crumple. It was summer
in Arkansas. What humidity,

these children, full of water. I hit him
also with the frying pan. I hit him

also with the guitar. We laughed later:
Where had the guitar come from? My dad

was a star collapsing. The first thing
a dying star does is swell—swallows

whatever is near. He tried to take us
into his body, which was the house

the police entered. This is how I knew
he was dying. I'd called the police.

What is your name? He tried to put us through
the walls of the house the police entered,

which was his body. *What is your name?*
Compromised: the integrity of a body

contracting. *What is your name, sir?* He answered:
Cronos. He answered: *I'm hungry.* He answered:

A god long dead. He threw up all his children
right there on the carpet. After all,

we were so small, the children. The thing
about a star collapsing is that it knows

neither that it is a star nor in collapse.
Everything is stardust, everything essential.

What is your name? Everything is resisting
arrest. Its gravity crushes the children

and the cruiser's rear passenger window.
The officer didn't know the star's name.

White dwarf? Black hole? To see: throw the collapsing
star face-first into anything. Face-first

into the backseat. Face-first into the pepper
spray. Face-first onto the precinct lawn.

Did you know you could throw a star? Do you
understand gravity, its weaknesses?

*You are in my house. You should already
know my name.*

Now

Dear—

don't forget   remember

remember your wife

Dear—

I am neither land nor timber, neither are you
ocean nor celestial body. Rather,
we are the small animals we've always been.

Land and sea know each other at the threshold
where they meet, as we know something of one
another, having shown, at different times,

some bit of flesh, some feeling. We called the showing
knowing instead of *practice*. We said,
at different times, *A feeling comes.*

What is the metaphor for two animals
sharing the same space? *Marriage?* We shared
a practice, a series of postures. See

how I became a tree [   ],
and you [   ] a body in space?

Sighting: Virtue

Rivergate Skate Center, Nashville, Tennessee

The man in orbit blooms
a heart on his back.

The heart blooms
wings of water, and in me rises

not mercy, but a sense of order.

I've drifted,
loosed from the one who bound me,

a planet with no anchoring star,
and I know this man

is neither god
nor sidereal body,

but neither is he a woman
with an alchemical heart.

His skin, his beard, his full breast
enrapture me,

draw my gaze
from every other whirling body.

I've drifted, and I know
the man in orbit is not a man

in orbit, but one in revolution,
where *revolution* means "change"

or "a way of moving,"
where muscle ripples to water,

moves from a state of gold
to one of lead.

Dear—

Your voice, broken as a body when you
speak of loss—of losing her—awash in
the grief that comes, I know, when the one you
love lets go and it is nothing you've done.

This morning I dreamed again of birds, blue
and dead, wings lifted in a parody
of flight—and yes, I'd sworn off the birds, love,
so they died, as any living thing might.

That's one reading, I suppose, another
way of letting go after having held
you once, for a while, content with the shape
of what was. Perhaps the birds were

an augury from myth, but who knows what
promise will rise or perish come morning?

Dear—

What will it take to dull me now, my breath
heavy beneath the weight of your cat
on my chest? I call, wait for confirmation,
your voice. Try not to imagine

your mouth on her mouth, your ring glinting
in some dim light, cool against her face,
her neck. You do not answer. You do not call.
I am an overreaction: a boil

of skin and itch and breath hitched like a child
realizing it is lost. Dear god, when
will you find a time for me? I take the pill.
Feed the cats, and bed down the dogs.

I hold my breath. My body hollows,
grows teeth: gathers bone, gathers root and nerve.

Hymn

Dear river dear creek dear dammed
tributaries dear fuse dear dynamite
and wet match. Amen.

The water don't love me and she don't love
me and maybe I'm drowning
from the inside.

            Who put the river
in my arm said *don't*
let the water?
            Maybe the knife

got a hard kiss and a sweet bite.
Maybe the knife only metal
and wood and a bit of brass

but maybe it know
how to love the inside of me.
Maybe I don't believe in meaning in god

in plans in paths and the closer I am
to my animal self the more human I am
the more I let myself break

            like a wave. Ocean
in my arm. Stone in my arm.
Iron and wood and brass in my arm.

Sighting: Tarot

Pflugerville, Texas

I learned how to hug here,
how to draw a boundary and hold
here against the gale force

of my mother's late-night rage
and sob; learned too what it meant
to be chosen, to choose. Brought myself

back to the receiving line, my chest cracked
into two wet pieces after a fall
so lonesome I wasn't sure I'd survive,

and met the arms practiced
in mending. I asked Jenny to read my cards,
Syd and Shannon on the couch

behind me, Amber and Jo in the kitchen,
Nat in from Berkeley, the kids
running around, Carlisha, I'm sure,

at my right hand. Jenny spread
the Celtic cross, gestured, as she does,
which is to say grandly, at my present,

at the problem we all knew, the past,
the conscious and unconscious, waited
for the cards to name what we could all see,

there at position of hopes and fears:
three swords in one heart.
How rude, I thought.

Do y'all see this shit?
I said aloud, the room gone quiet,

a relief not to have to say what I had known
in the room where I'd learned the kind
of love possible between friends,

now family, the kindness possible
between partners—grateful for the rough blow,
finally landed, and the net to catch me.

Dear—

Question: How do we process being overcome
when we know the water is rising, rising
because the sea ice is melting, melting
because the animal we are shortens
everything we touch into brief, useful
pieces? Question: Can we call our marriage
done, soon overcome, soon underwater,
a city inhabited by whatever
the sea brings to it? Question: How do you drown
a city? Throw into the ocean
every suffocation: the folded clothes,
the lemon tree, a wife. Anything
that will sink as a stone. Dear one, is it too soon
to call? I cannot swim, and I will not drown.

Dear—

What nerve—

        what mucus and bone.

The sea cannot walk

                away. I know

    the shore cannot walk

                away. I know

      the redwood—

           the heartwood—

needs fire,

      water too,

          and space.

    They cannot walk away

             but must grow

  so far

        apart.

    Mark the rings,

         cored:

how long we lasted.

         That year: famine;

      this year:

           smoke;

what opened

        in the flame.

Now
|
Then

Dear—

████████████████████████████████████

████████████████████████████████████

████████████████████████████████████

████████████████████████████████████

███████████████████████████████ I wanted
to forget so many things. ████████████████

████████████████████████████████████

████████████████████████████████████

████████████████████████████████████

████████████████████████████████████

████████████████████████████████████

████████████████████████████████████

████████████████████████████████████

████████████████████████████████████

████████████████████████████████████

████████████████████████████████████

████████████

Self-Portrait in Labyrinth

Northern California, 2016

We sit in the sun, knees up, and perhaps
there is an ocean if we are feeling

small—a field of birds shaken like a wet
sheet toward the sky if we are well. We come

to these places slowly, try to see what
is in front of us: a robin, the cat's-

ear or hawk's-beard, the harbor seals blobbing
the beach, or an otter making good use

of the pier in the late afternoon light.
We lose hold, sometimes, of the field, the ocean,

slip into the labyrinth of our one self.
Sometimes, the labyrinth is like the field,

the walls set far apart, and we don't know
that we are lost until we find we cannot

sit as we are accustomed—pushed forward
by the roar of the beast whose home this is,

our guts rattled, the wide lane shook. There is
no golden thread, but we remember each

turn, each stone the mortar sets; we remember
when he built this maze inside of us,

unfolded himself to sit now at the center;
we remember, or try, the schooling birds,

their wingbeat a heart at rest; we remember,
or try, the salt wind. We fear there is a way

out, through the trembling corridor, the center—
the beast finally asleep—the scattered

bones—the beast before us. Whose face will it
wear? What good use will we make of our hands?

The Oracle Remembers the Future Cannot Be Avoided

Magnolia, Arkansas, 2002

The oracle wakens as the daughter does,
at the phone ringing, a landline, next to the bed,

her *Hello mama*, overridden
by the mother, drunk again and crying.

The oracle tries not to listen, to silence,
to refuse, but the mother is loud,

the mother like a siren
dashing the daughter

against the question:

Did Daddy [   ]?

The daughter's panic touches the oracle,
even as it wonders which answer

the daughter will give, even as it wonders
why the mother calls the father *Daddy*,

even as it remembers

the mother—

a child—

1970 and still Arkansas:
everywhere a blanket of wet,

mosquitoes. Open windows,
open eyes, and the man come to shake the foot

of the childmother's bed. The oracle thinks, *Run*,
but the childmother's leg doesn't move.

The oracle thinks, *Hide*, but where?

The childmother is just a girl and dark
and the man carries her into the high grass to split her—

The oracle and daughter make a similar calculus.
Though the daughter soothes the mother,

the oracle knows the soothing to be short lived,
knows the daughter will call back,

the call a sword: a key: a thread
throwing its light into the room.

Self-Portrait with Door

Compton, California, early 1990s

Do you remember the princess
locked in a tower, a doorless room
because her father feared a grandson
who might kill him? And the god, who slid
into her room as light as rain as gold,
a deluge she bore and later bore him
a son who would kill a king?

Well, this is not that.

A girl awakens in a room, the door
unpainted, with no knob—just a hole
where the knob could be. Eyes closed,
she imagines the lock. She imagines
locking herself inside. She imagines
her father knocking, the lock a rebuke.
Imagines his disappointment at the door,
which cannot yield. Imagines sleeping
through the night. Imagines him still,
standing at the locked door.

This is still not that.

I open my eyes. He is standing
at the foot of my bed. He has pushed
the open door, pushed open the room
as a man. Tonight, he will pin me
to a wall in the open room, frottage
between my thighs, and I will bear him.

Another night, he will take me
in the kitchen and I will bear him;
or the laundry room and I will bear him;
or the bedroom he shares with my mother.

I will bear him wherever I am taken
and no one will kill him and he will not die.

Mounting Dead Butterflies Is Not Hard

My child hunger, my child body, all need—
arch and alpha and shameless in the dark—
ground against any nearly hard thing:

faces of my stuffed animals, girl
cousins, my own hardening bones, breathless
and panting in the hunt for my own slick

pleasure. I say *shameless* when I mean *unshamed*,
my parents' failure to curb to bind to strike
each *nasty* act, my wild hunt. Unshameable

until my father
                  mounted me, an insect
pinned to the walls, the kitchen tile.

I say *my father.*
I say *wall* and *tile.*

I say *mount.*
I say *me.*

I keep looking away.

Better the dried wing, dried ganglia,
useless nerve cord. Better the small body

in the boiled water, disinfected and softened
in the airtight container of the poem.

Better the wings pinned between corkboard
and paper, dried again in a warm room,

ready to be mounted under glass
with a pin through the thorax.

Better that than to remember,
even once, what shames me:

my child brain and mammal body, my
hunting hips, my face in my father's neck.

Self-Portrait with Father

We sit on opposite sides of a picnic bench,
behind him, the black walnut tree, its fruit

rich with maggots. Behind me, a wall of ivy
we prune every other season. I've called

this Saturday morning meeting,
the sun already hard, the air dry.

I say to my father, who I call *Dad*,
that his mama, a woman I've never met—

who died when he was two years older
than I am in this memory—I argue

her disappointment. His head hangs
like a limb at the truth, his hands sweeping

down his mustache, his lips before he nods,
says, *I don't know why I keep [   ]*.

I am all hope, the choice in that moment
so simple a child could figure it, and I say,

You can stop.

Does he nod again? Or sit still or move
his eyes to the swing set,

the dog asleep beneath the olive tree?
I can't remember.

I only know he fails, holds me
to every wall in the house again and again.

Apologia

I

It begins as no apologia does: with an apology \\ a desire to
offer something in return \\ for what was taken \\ under
the black walnut tree \\ over the maggot fruit \\ in the peach
room \\ the door with no knob \\ the door unpainted \\ in the
kitchen \\ the linoleum worn and gold \\ in my parents' bedroom
\\ in the den \\ in the dining room \\ in the living room \\ or
anywhere \\ we've been alone \\ *is his hat* \\ *in his hand* \\ he
doesn't wear a hat \\ *I meant it metaphorically* \\ still he
apologized \\ still he said he was sorry \\ still he offered me
anything I wanted \\ he asked what I wanted \\ but what had he
taken \\ what \\ what \\ what could he give me in return?

II

He sits in the passenger seat of my
1985 Honda Prelude. I am

looking forward, toward the shed of the house
I used to live in, a house more than

two thousand miles away from where he
[   ] me. Inside, my mother

spins, a tornado smashing her children
into refuse. Who remembers when last

she was sober? Who remembers? Outside,
in my car, one headlight held up with bungee

cord and hook, I ask my dad, I say, [

                              ]?
He looks forward. He is too big for this car.

His hands, scarred and callused, haven't been clean
for longer than I can remember.

I remember how high he would throw the ball.
I remember him picking me up

when I was asleep, how safe, then unsafe
I felt. All the ways he carried me away.

He is sorry for [   ] me,
but he will not admit [   ] me

to anyone outside this car. Not to
my aunts or great-aunts, not to my grandfather

or mother, who, though they believe any man
capable, though they know what he has done,

crowd into the space his denial makes.
Still, he convinces me a second time.

No argument but the apology:
voice low, his hands dirty in his own lap.

III

The small shames \\ are the hardest to say \\ we went to the toy
store \\ I picked out a small model plane \\ the rubber cement \\ I
remember the paints were too expensive \\ so \\ no paint \\ *what
did your brother and sister get* \\ *no way you got a toy* \\ *and
they nothing* \\ Paperboy on the radio \\ Too $hort \\ the sun
shining on our way to the mall \\ on the way back \\ fucking
California sun \\ the plane the only thing I could think to say \\ I
had wanted it \\ or something like it \\ for so long \\ so frivolous
\\ the plane \\ with no paint \\ that I put together the rest
of the afternoon \\ what he gave me in return.

IV

Now the apologia, said not to me
in the faint flickering of his half-life.

We have not spoken in ten years,
which means he does not walk into my room

unbidden, does not stand just inside my
open door, his body swayed and swaggered,

beer rimming his breath. He does not
wheel his gaze in my direction, does not say,

> *I am not \\ sorry \\ I liked it \\ I would \\ do*
> *it again \\ if I had the chance \\ again \\ if I*
> *had the chance \\ again \\ I am not sorry \\ I*
> *am not sorry \\ not \\ sorry \\ not sorry.*

The drunken slur of a man once confused
for a god for a father, bellowing

for what he no longer has: belief
and worship, the fat and the bone,

the flower-wreathed daughter
tossed at his feet.

The Oracle Remembers the Future Cannot Be Avoided

Magnolia, Arkansas, 2002

Not now, the oracle whispers, perhaps
out for a night walk in a place so overcast

that even moonlight is precious. Even
an oracle cannot choose what or how

to remember. Still, it's so maudlin,
the woman in bed drinking orange juice

and eating Tylenol in twos and threes.
The lava lamp her father gave her

years before pulsing a slick blue light
against the walls of her room in a house

that once belonged only to her and her
uncle, before her sister's boyfriend,

and then her sister, moved in; before
the uncle and the sister's boyfriend

started selling crack from the uncle's bedroom
window; before her mother threatened,

every weekend, to call the police
on the uncle and boyfriend for selling crack;

the threat blanketing the house, including
the woman on the bed who'd betrayed the mother

by admitting the father made use
of her body when the daughter was a child.

And why wouldn't the mother punish them all,
gather them in hand to disappear?

The oracle, lost for a moment
in the mother, returns to the woman

on the bed, with her Tylenol and orange
juice, her failing peristalsis, the lamp's

blue light, and Oprah, with that voice like wealth,
like control, reading *White Oleander,*

abridged, on audiobook. How old is she?
Nineteen? That seems right—

                                  well, none of this is right,

but *this is how it ends*, the woman thinks.
Only the oracle knows the woman

will wake hours later, will crawl toward
the narrow hall, over its brown indoor-outdoor

carpet, and puke up the juice and pills
just outside the bathroom door.

The oracle knows, too, that the sister will
clean the mess, will wipe the woman's mouth

with a damp cloth and help her back to bed,
and the woman will wake again,

and for the rest of her life, in regret
that she had nothing stronger to take.

Now

Dear—

████████████

████████████████████████████

████████████████████████████████

████████████████████████████████

███████████████████████████

████████████

████████ *what am I doing* █████████

████████████████████████████████

████████████████████████████████

████████████████████████████████

████████████████████████████

████████████████ I say to myself █████ *Please forgive me.*
I love you. █████████████████████

████████████████████

████████████████████████████████

████████ Me, me, me. █████████████████

████████████████████████████████████

████████████████████████████

████████████████████████████████

████████████████ I'm going to work ██████████

████████████

Dear—

I take the first snowfall for ash. Mistake,
I mean, the first flake that comes wisping
down for the remnant of some thing burned,
perhaps, for warmth or in error. When we were
young, we stood with our backs not to the past
or future but toward the hot desperation
of being alive and for right now.
At the canyon's edge, the wind, thick as a hand,
readied to push you into gorge and river
rock. *Come back*, I said. And the wind took
my voice too. Love, there is no fire here—
only water, finally, drifting
to coat the grass, to keep it green, to heap
the limbs and needles in wet, heavy white.

Where I End Up

Western New York

We pushed through high desert into a new
wilderness, the air filling with water

and timber and rich earth the farther east
we went—too far and older than anywhere

I've ever lived and riven with loneliness.
At night and alone, I imagine the ghosts

this place carries pushing through the earth
like water. I wonder whether the ones

I carry will find a home here, or if
they will wander with me, faithful and true.

What I bring, I've always had: a dull knife,
a child afraid of the night and herself,

the woman you left. Still, there's only doing
and done, the same sun, and who can remember home?

I wasn't born haunted

I. *Visitation*

The double-spouted, horse-haired wedding vase,
given to us by your aunt and uncle, the one you packed
with my things, carefully wrapped, and exiled
as I was exiled, fell twice from the closet
shelf before it broke. That was the summer
I dreamed of a girl in white who told me
she had haunted this town since 1854.
The town was founded on oil and timber,
a promised canal from lake to river,
but I felt the blood in it. All through the fall—the months
I waited for winter, then the months of winter—I lived
with the violence of all that had been taken here,
such that, come summer, whatever rattled
the living room walls, I turned my back,
thought, *if it needs me, it will call my name.*

II. *I'm sorry, the girl said from inside the closet*

Everything dead was once living.
I remember how like the land we became:
the groundwater pumped dry,
us settling into subsidence.

We almost survived the drought we'd wandered into,
but found the water too late,
the dust too thick.

I don't believe in ghosts,
which doesn't mean they aren't real.

The second fall,
despite your careful wrapping,
broke one of the spouts clean off.

I figured this was one way of calling my name,
of saying *enough*.

Sighting: Almost

Vernal Fall, Yosemite National Park

Never mind the 600 stairs carved in granite
or my guide, a man with a mustache
and no concept of *almost*, or my moaned

why are we going up this hill, at every hill,
or his response that *what comes up
must go down*, or the somewhere

we've almost reached. Mind instead
the three friends who breached
the safety rail for a picture on the rocks

and were swept over the falls by a river
gorged with the melting snowpack.
How they must have held each other

in their descent before the Merced
broke them apart.
That was some time ago.

An old man hiking with his son-in-law
flatters me, *You are only pretending
to be tired to make us feel*

better. The truth: I have come here
to learn how not to kill myself.
My guide takes my picture many times

as we ascend. He captures Half Dome,
El Capitan, Nevada Fall, and me, nearly
upright, a silhouette before the sun.

Sighting: Rockfall

John Muir Trail, Yosemite National Park

Descent should be easy, but the granite
molted like thunder and undid the trail.

The root: water and winter, then spring
and water. The bloom: a cleaving.

I picked over the rocks and broken
boughs, the ground mulched soft.

I carried her to the mouth
of the trail when I meant to recover

only myself. You see, I was the ghost,
and she rose to sing, to be torn to pieces.

Partial Hospitalization

The bird I drew
much larger than it should have been
because it lived inside me:

purple head, blue neck, green belly,
bright orange tail.

Imagine a dinosaur living inside
your breast, beating
like a heart where your heart
should be—

I promised I wouldn't think
of birds, of what hollowed
my chest, of what I tried to let loose
through the small doors of my wrists.

I promised no new doors
into my body.

I promised a body free
of fossils buried in the bone
like the rings of a tree—

Look,
it got away from me:
the bird,
the dinosaur.

The cloaca: an opening
in the body to expel waste, eggs, sperm.

Imagine your chest
full of waste beating like a wave
all over itself.
Not waste but wings.

The bird painted with chalk.
The background muddled blue and green and gray.
The background ugly so the bird might fly.

A dead thing that, in dying, feeds the living

I've been thinking about the anatomy
of the egg, about the two interior membranes,

the yolk held in place by the chalazae, gases
moving through the semipermeable shell.

A curious phrase, *the anatomy of the egg*,
as if an egg were a body, which it is,

as if the egg could be broken then mended,
which, depending on your faith, broken yes,

but mended? Well. Best to start
again, with a new body, voided

from a warmer one, brooded and turned.
Better to begin as if some small-handed

animal hadn't knocked you against a rock,
licked clean the rich yolk and left

the albumen to dry in the sun—as if a hinged
jaw hadn't swallowed you whole.

What I wanted: a practice that reassured
that what was cracked could be mended

or, at least, suspended so that it could not spread.
But now I wonder: better to be the egg or scaled

mandible? The small hand or the flies, bottle black
and green, spilling their bile onto whatever's left,

sweeping the interior, drinking it clean?
I think, *Something might have grown there*, though

I know it was never meant to be eaten;
it was always meant to spoil.

Dear—

I saw the crow first, on the shoulder turned
to mud, then its shadow, then the cage

of bone arcing up from the muck. April
thaw, the doe untagged, head intact—the rope

looped about her neck, blue and man-made.
Below the neck, the body emptied,

the muscle inexpertly butchered, no
doubt, in some dark hollow, the ribs scraped

a dirty gray—gristle and fat, the remnants.
Look: all of this was out of season, the doe

tossed on the roadside, the melted snow—
even me, standing over the carcass

and why? The crow long gone now, and what
marked the line between winter and spring?

After

The moon rose over the bay. I had a lot of feelings.

The home I've been making inside myself started
with a razing, a brush clearing, the thorn and nettle,
the blackberry bush falling under the bush hog.

Then I rested, a cycle fallow. Said *winter.* Said *the ground
is too cold to break, pony.* Said *I almost set fire
to it all, lit a match, watched it ghost in the wind.*

Came the thaw, came the melting snowpack, the flooded river,
new ground water, the well risen. I stood in the mud field
and called it a pasture. Stood with a needle in my mouth

and called it a song. Everything rushed past my small ears:
whir in the leaves, whir in the wing and the wood. *About time
to get a hammer,* I thought. *About time to get a nail and saw.*

Notes

"Ars Empathica": An early draft of this poem was a part of an exchange between the writer and visual artist Susanna Kwan and me. In 2013 and 2014, we maintained a correspondence by mail in which she would send me a drawing that I would respond to with a poem. She would then create a drawing in response to the poem and send that to me, and I would write a poem in response to that image. Thus began a kind of exquisite conversation, a call and response, an infinite and distorting mirror.

"Sanctuary": An early draft of this poem was a part of the exchange with Susanna Kwan.

"Dear— (What nerve—)": An early draft of this poem came out of a writing prompt that students in my poetry workshop at St. Bonaventure University designed. The exercise was in response to Christopher Soto's poems in *Subject to Change: Trans Poetry & Conversation*, edited by H. Melt.

"Mounting Dead Butterflies Is Not Hard": The title is taken from the now defunct site *Butterfly Fun Facts* (www.butterfly-fun-facts.com), where Edith Ellen Smith continues, "At least, not the most casual method of mounting."

"I wasn't born haunted": According to the City of Olean's municipal webpage on the town's history: "Olean was incorporated as a village and granted its first charter by the legislature in 1854."

"Sighting: Almost": In the summer of 2011, Hormiz David, Ninos Yacoub, and Ramina Badal died after entering the water above Vernal Fall in Yosemite National Park. One slipped, and when the other two tried to save her, they were all swept over the falls, which were particularly strong because of a melting, heavy snowpack. None of them survived.

"A dead thing that, in dying, feels the living": In the summer of 2017, I participated in a workshop at the Fine Arts Work Center led by Gabrielle Calvocoressi. This poem came out of an exercise Gaby gave us early in the week.

"The moon rose over the bay. I had a lot of feelings.": This poem came out of a prompt Gaby gave us on the second day of our workshop. Gaby credited Rita Dove as the originator of the prompt, a version of which you can find in *The Practice of Poetry*, edited by Robin Behn and Chase Twichell.

Acknowledgments

I'm grateful to the editors of the following publications for publishing earlier versions of these poems.

The Adroit Journal, "Sighting: Almost" and "Sighting: Rockfall" (as "Sighting: Avalanche")

Black Warrior Review, "Portrait of My Father as a Winged Boar," "Oracle," and "The moon rose over the bay. I had a lot of feelings."

BuzzFeed, "Partial Hospitalization"

The Cincinnati Review, "Hymn"

Foglifter, "Where I End Up"

The New Yorker, "From *The Catalogue of Cruelty*"

The Paris Review, "Dear— (I saw the crow first)"

Poetry, "A dead thing that, in dying, feeds the living" and "Dear— (I am neither land nor timber)"

Poetry Now, "Sanctuary"

The Rumpus, "Sighting: Virtue"

The Sewanee Review, "Dear—(We come from abundance)," "Dear— (I take the first snowfall)," and "Continental Drift Theory"

Sinister Wisdom, "Bedtime Story for the Bruised-Hearted" and "Cartography as an act of remembering"

Tin House, "The Oracle Remembers the Future Cannot Be Avoided (*Los Angeles, California, 1970s*)"

Washington Square, "In the Chapel of St. Mary's" and "Self-Portrait in Labyrinth"

"Cartography as an act of remembering" was reprinted in the anthology *Furious Flower: Seeding the Future of African American Poetry*.

"Apologia" was first published in the anthology *Indelible in the Hippocampus: Writings from the Me Too Movement*.

"Sanctuary" was reprinted in the anthology *New Daughters of Africa: An International Anthology of Writing by Women of African Descent*.

Without the support of the following organizations, I would not have had the time, space, and experiences needed to write the poems in this collection: the Lannan Foundation, Cave Canem, the Fine Arts Work Center, the Constance Saltonstall Foundation for the Arts, St. Bonaventure University, Baruch College, the PSC-CUNY Cycle 50 Research Award Grant, and CUNY's Faculty Fellowship Publication Program. Thank you for your generosity and for trusting me with the space and resources necessary to do my work.

Thank you Jeff Shotts, Fiona McCrae, and the team at Graywolf for making a home for and taking such good care of this work.

The Courage to Heal: A Guide for Women Survivors of Child Sexual Abuse by Ellen Bass and Laura Davis and *The Courage to Heal Workbook: A Guide for Women and Men Survivors of Child Sexual Abuse* by Laura Davis were vital to my process in writing the poems for this collection. I am grateful, too, to all the therapists I've had over the last sixteen or so years, especially Heather Greenblatt and Barbara Danish, who, while I was writing these poems, helped me navigate and validate my feelings around having been abused as a child.

My immense gratitude to Elizabeth Barnett, Carlisha Bell, Destiny O. Birdsong, Ama Codjoe, and Ladan Osman for their friendship, for reading the manuscript in its several stages, and for providing such thoughtful feedback.

To my chosen family: thank you for loving me, and in loving me, for seeing me whole.

Melissa Febos, beloved and most dear, thank you for practicing with me such kindness, such gentleness, such sweetness and love.

Donika Kelly is a poet, Cave Canem graduate fellow, and member of the collective Poets at the End of the World. She is the author of *Bestiary*, which won the Cave Canem Poetry Prize, the Hurston/Wright Legacy Award, and the Kate Tufts Discovery Award, and was longlisted for the National Book Award. She teaches at the University of Iowa.

The text of *The Renunciations* is set in Minion Pro.
Book design by Rachel Holscher.
Composition by Bookmobile Design and Digital
Publisher Services, Minneapolis, Minnesota.
Manufactured by Sheridan Saline on acid-free,
100 percent postconsumer wastepaper.